Learning About Loss

Written By Brittany G. Cummings

Dedicated to my loving Daddy and Momma, Randall and Michelle. I love you both so much. Hugs, Kisses, Cool.

We all go through loss in life. Sometimes it's the death of our loving family pet, or sometimes it's the death of a close family member or friend. Coping with death in a healthy way is very important in life. So, how do we do that?

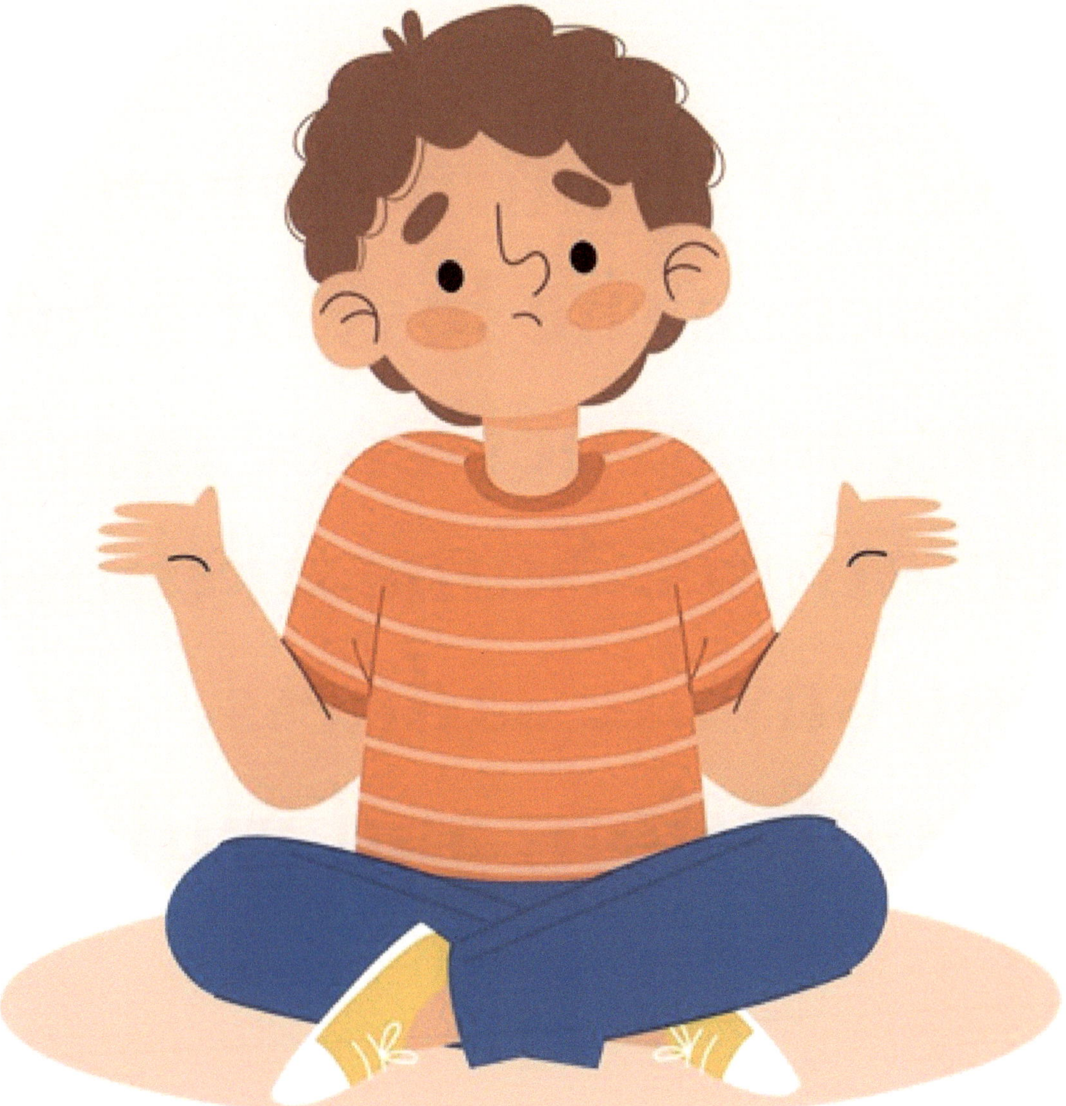

Most of the time when we experience the loss of a loved one, we experience many emotions. Some of those emotions are sadness, anger, confusion, and guilt.

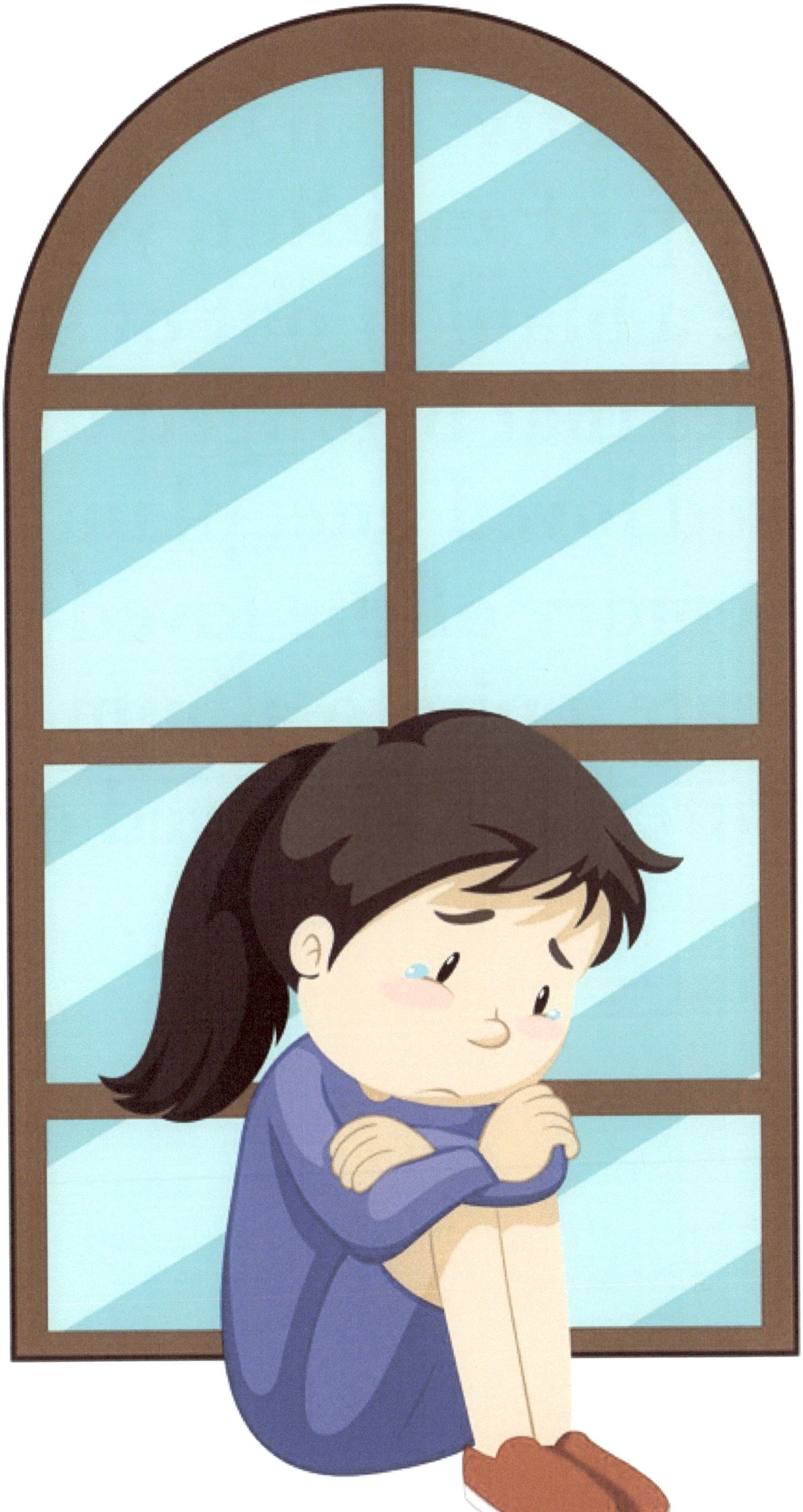

To cope with these feelings, being creative can help. With the help of an adult, you can make a blanket out of some clothes that belonged to the deceased loved one, plant a tree in memory of the loved one, or create a photo album with pictures of your loved one.

June 5, 2018

If you are involved in sports, focusing on the practices and games can help.

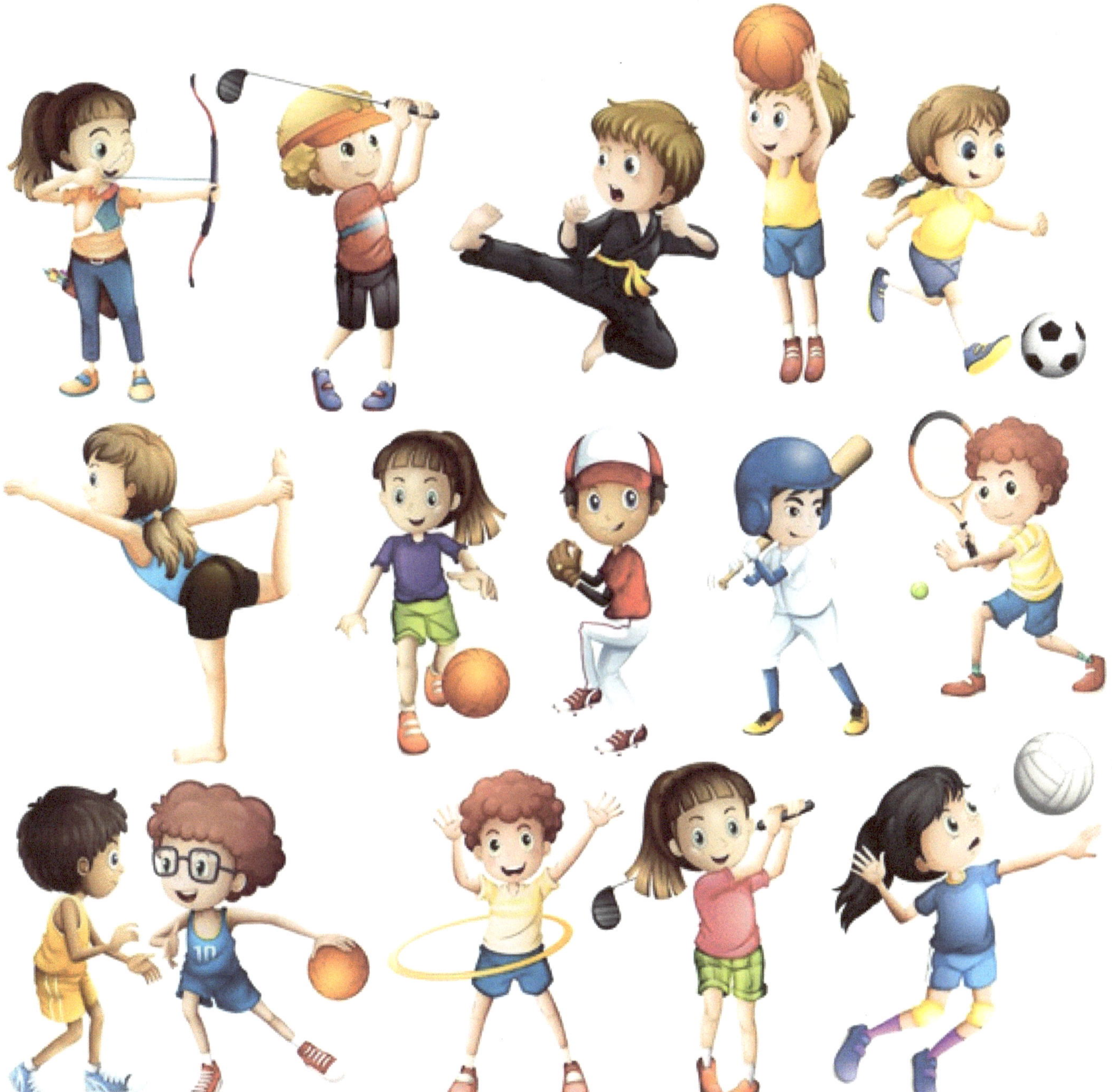

Try keeping a picture or word journal to cope with your feelings. Draw or write whatever comes to mind.

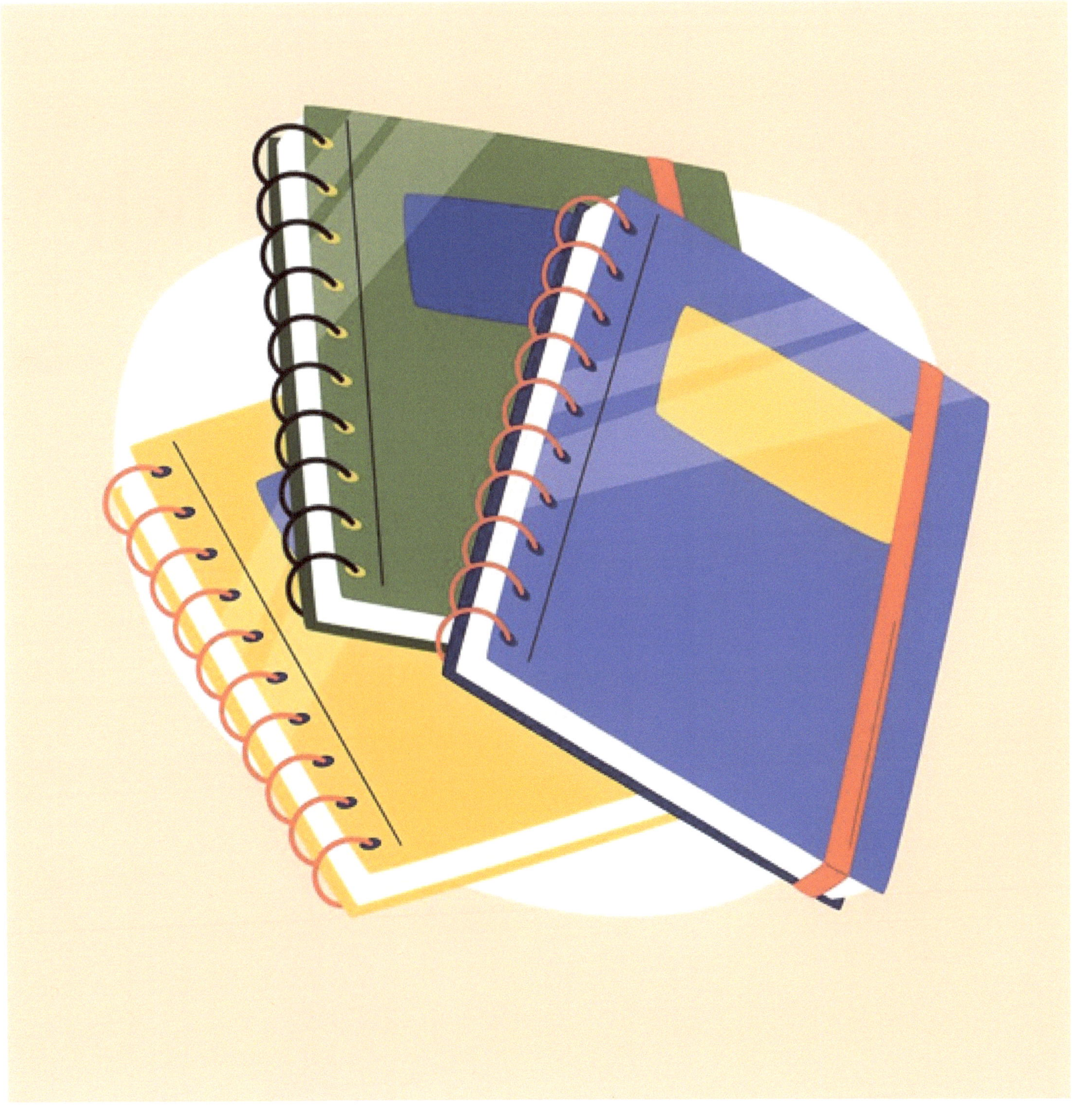

Listening to music can help you cope as well.

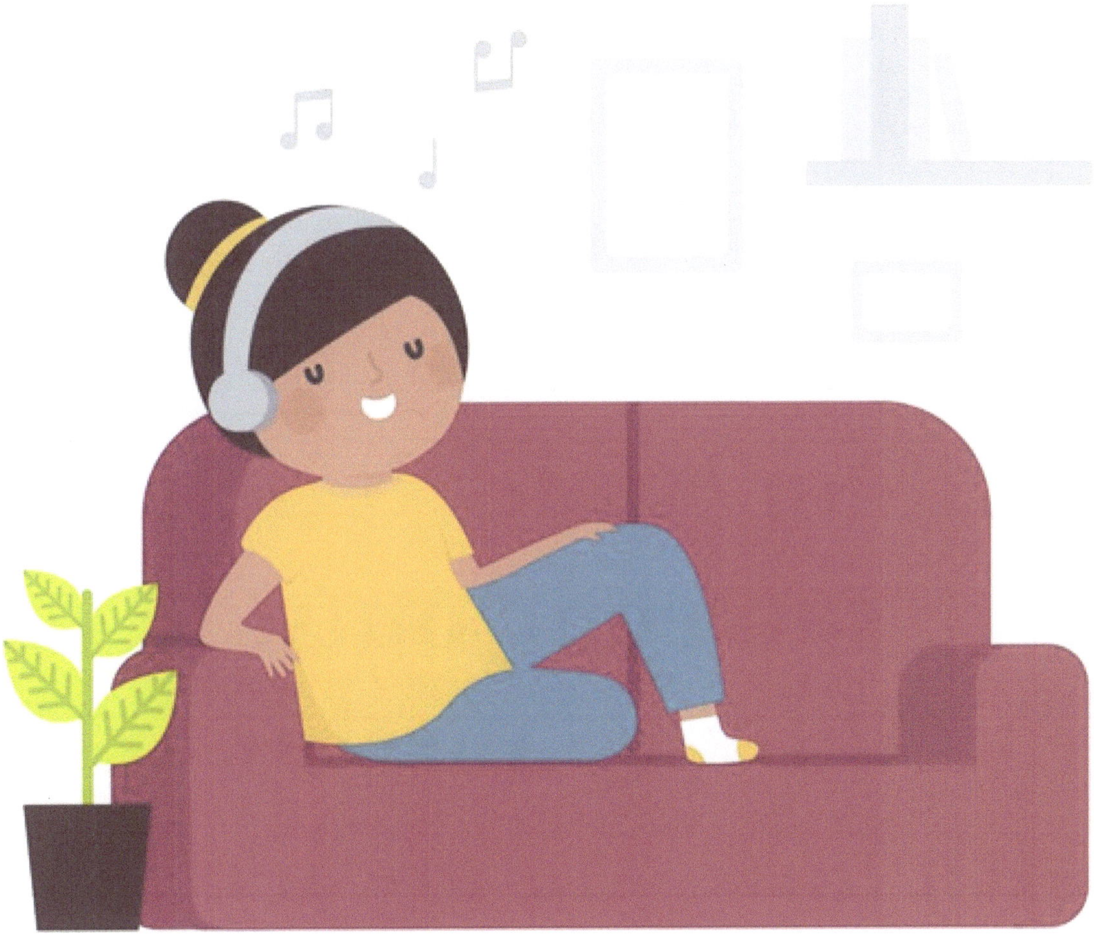

Sometimes, talking to someone you trust about how you feel can help. You can talk about memories of your loved one or look at pictures of the loved one. Sometimes it helps to talk to someone outside your family, like a counselor, to cope with how you are feeling.

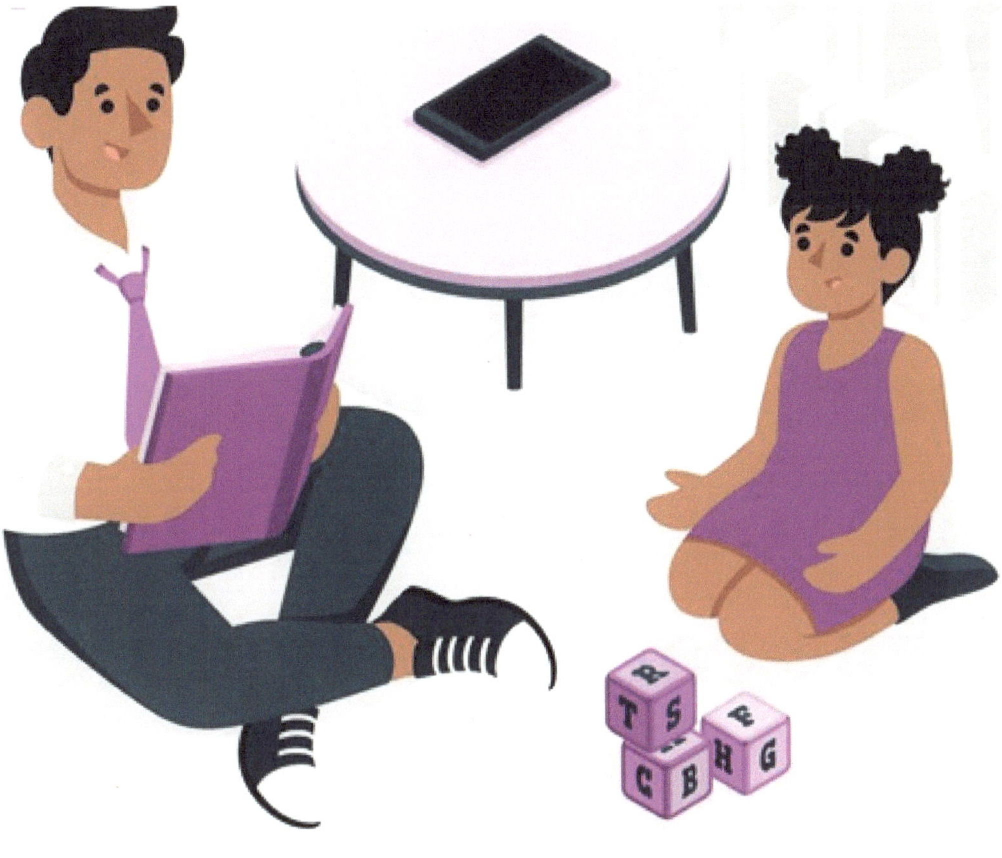

If you are feeling anger, talk to someone you trust about this anger. Maybe you feel anger towards that loved one. If you are feeling anger, talk to someone you trust about it. Maybe you feel anger towards someone completely different, and that's ok. Coping with that anger in a healthier way, will help you get through it.

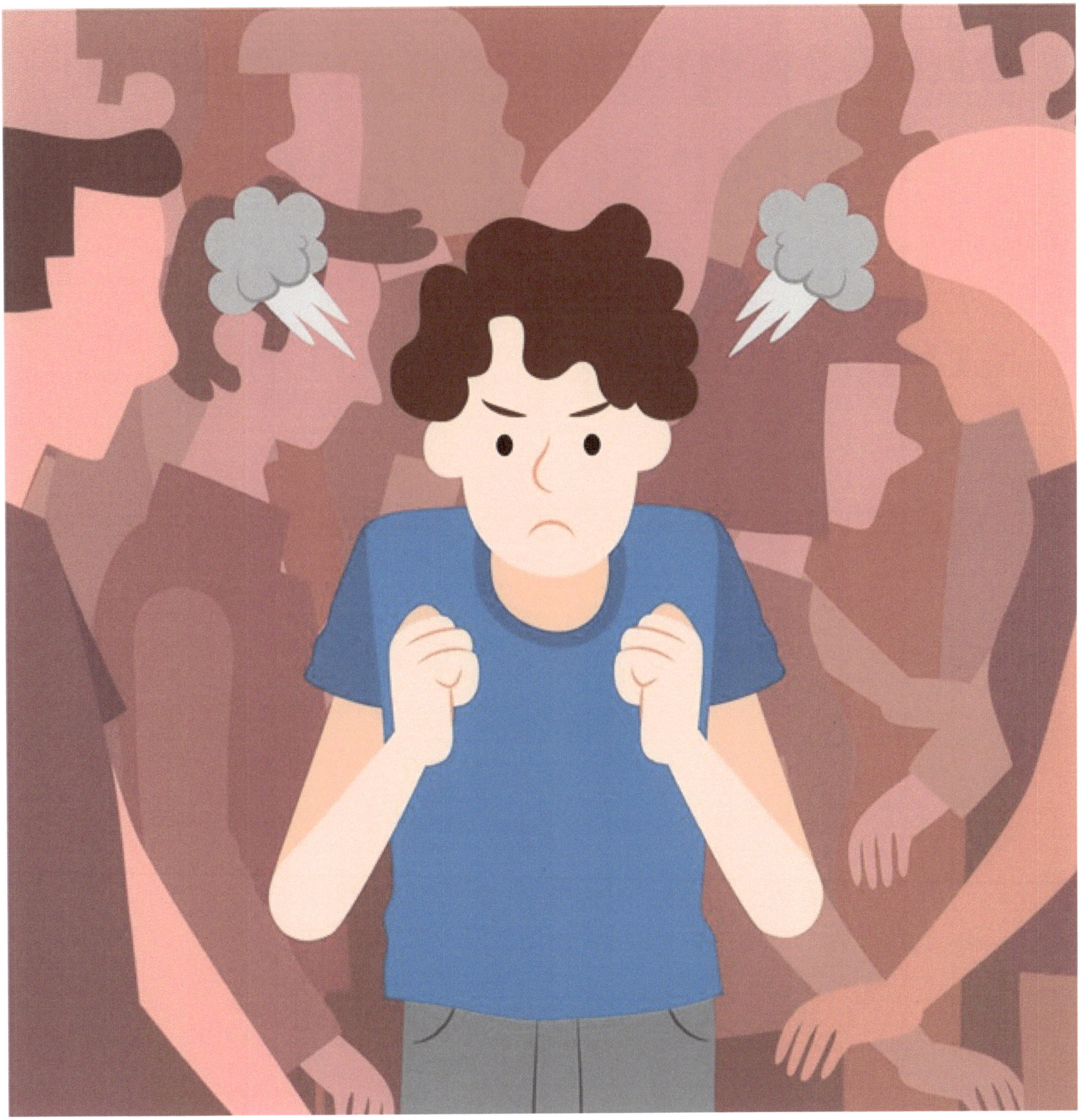

Getting cardboard boxes or old newspapers to stomp on and rip up can help you deal with your anger. You can even crumple up pieces of paper!

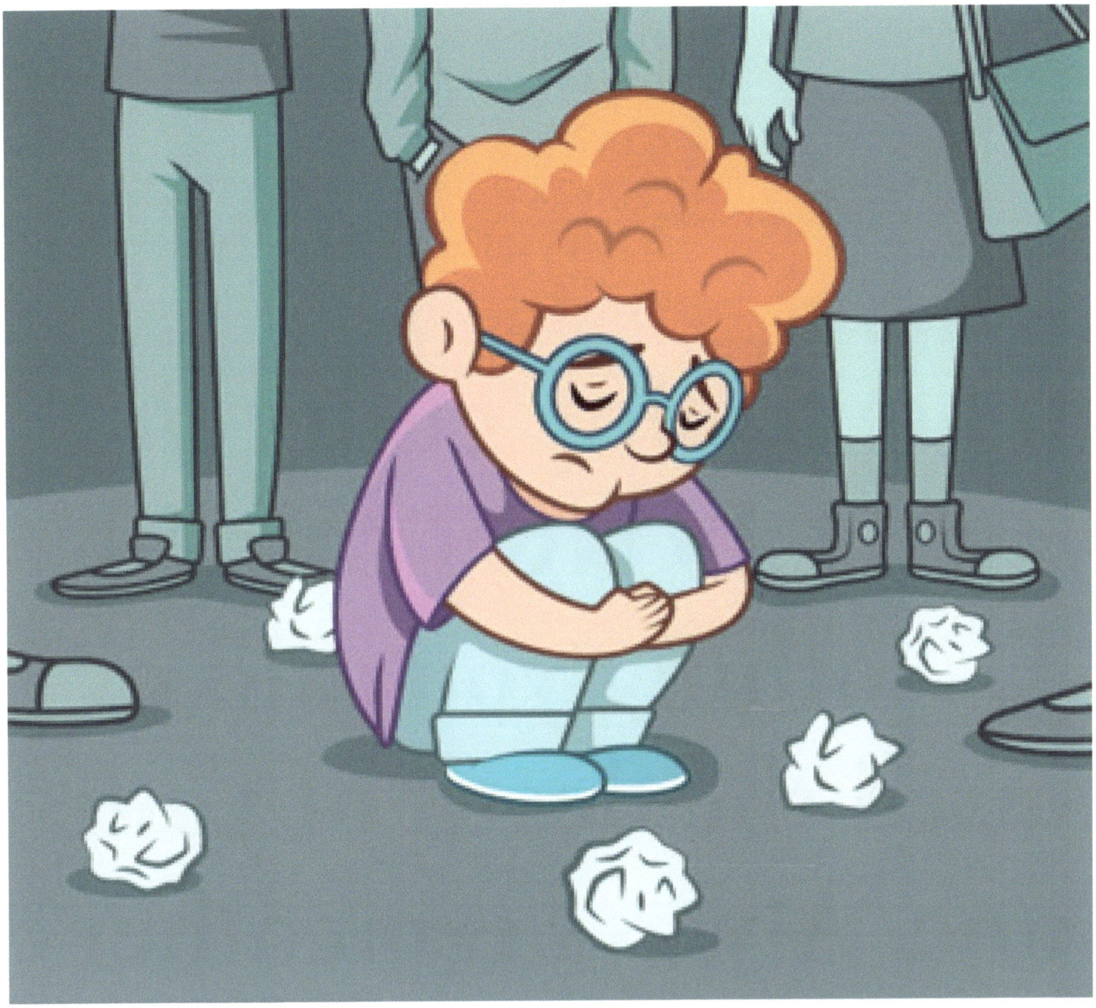

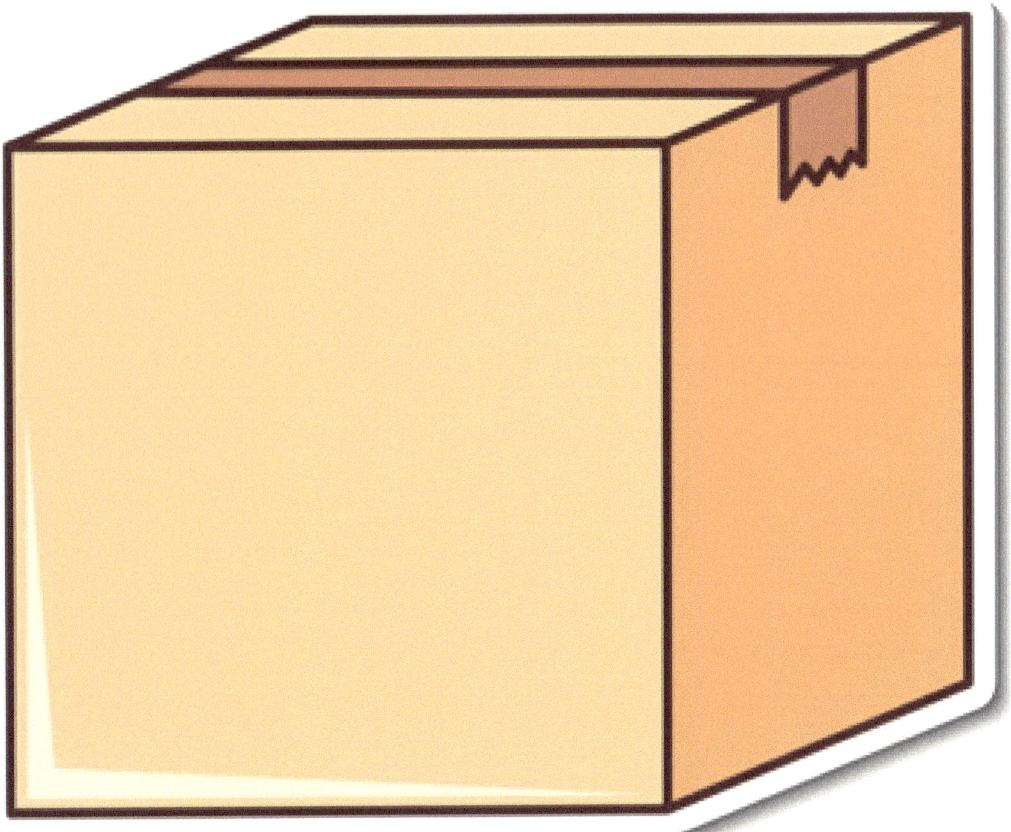

If you are feeling guilty in any way: IT IS NOT YOUR FAULT. Nothing you said or did, caused the death of your loved one. Always remember that.

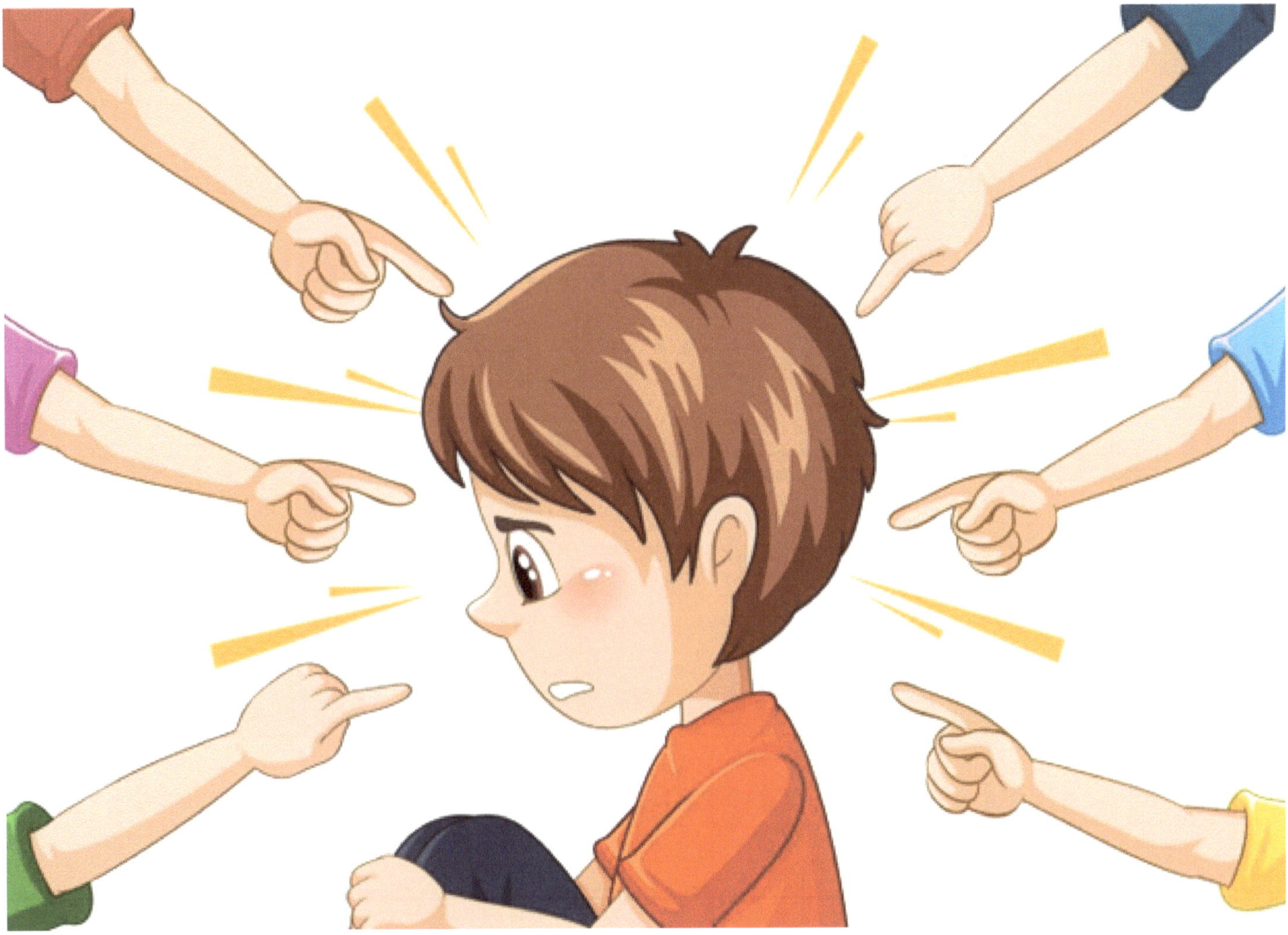

Sometimes after a loved one has passed, there will be a funeral, which is a celebration of the life they had and a way for some people to cope with the death of the loved one. Whether you attend the funeral or not is your choice. Whichever decision you make is the right decision.

If you choose to go to the funeral, it's good to know what to expect. There will most likely be many people crying. They're crying because that is how they are coping, at that moment with the sadness they are feeling.

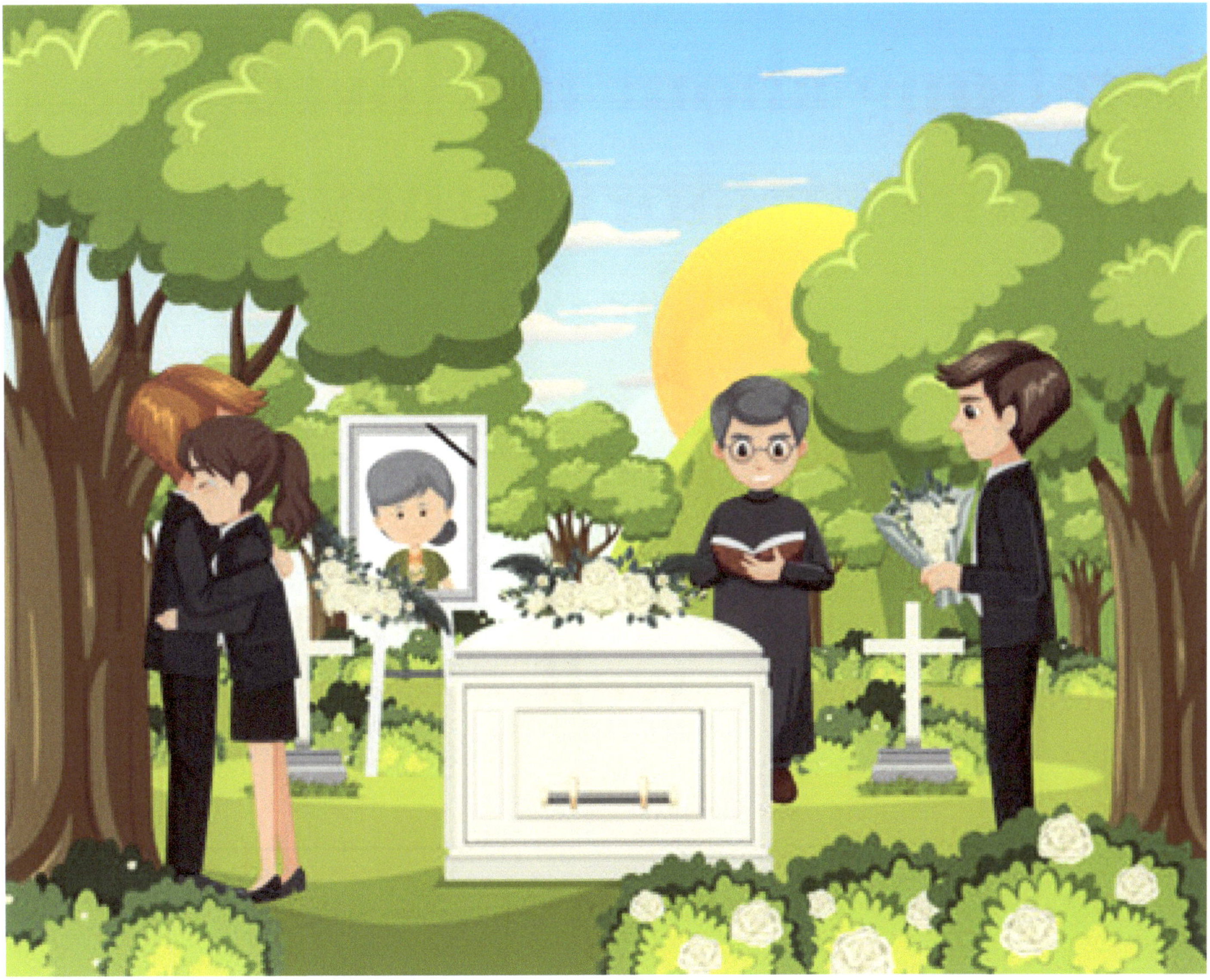

There will also be people talking about the loved one and the memories they have of them.

There will most likely be pictures of the loved one, as well.

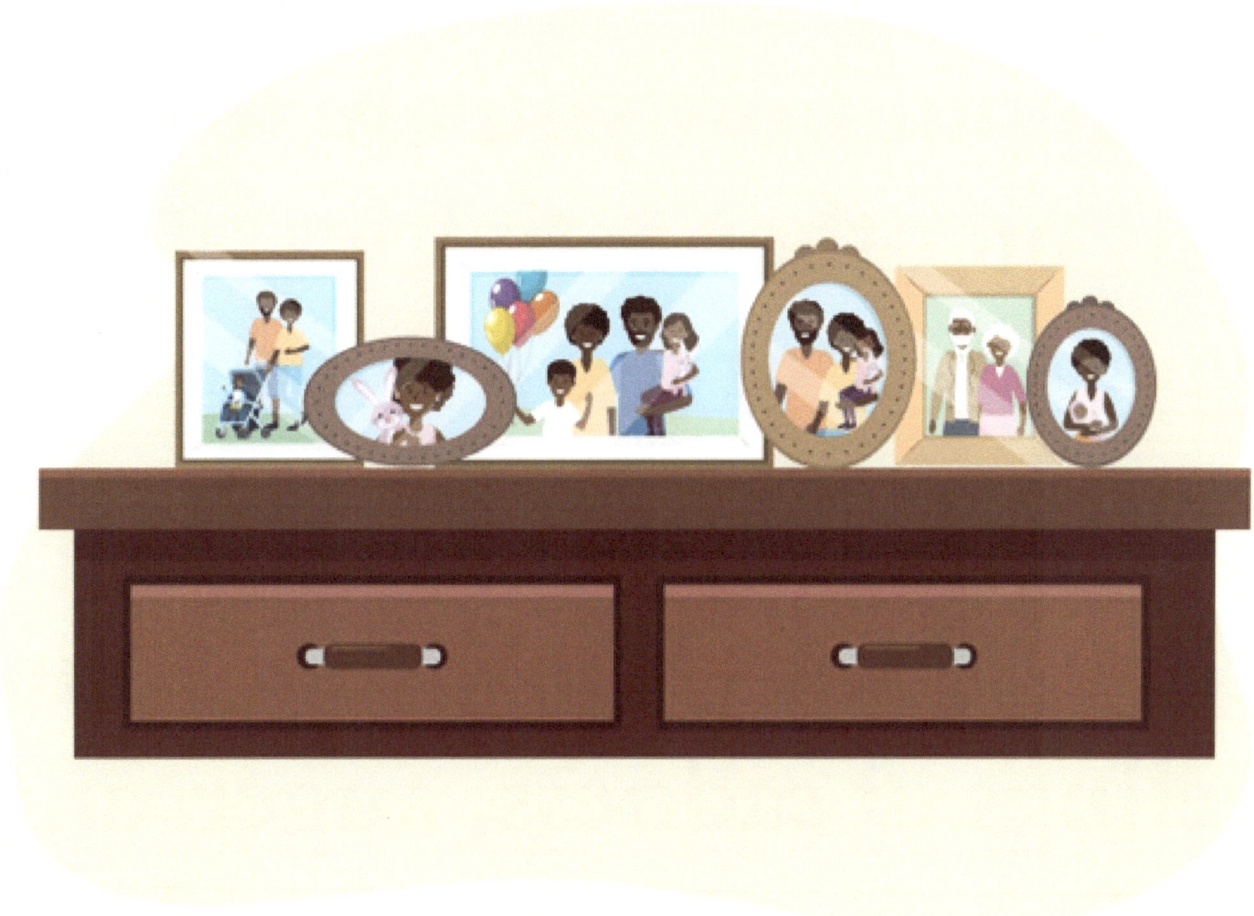

You are not alone in coping with the death of a loved one. You can talk to another loved one about how you are feeling, focus on other activities to help you cope, or keep a journal.

However you choose to cope, always know that your feelings of sadness, anger, and confusion are normal and ok.

You are not alone

About Brittany G. Cummings

My name is Brittany. Born and raised in East Tennessee. I'm a Jesus-follower, family loving, football and hockey fan.

I worked as a veterinary technician while I finished my psychology and English degrees from the University of Tennessee. I then worked as a counselor for children with mental health issues. Now, I have the best "job" in the world: stay-at-home-mom.

My story telling began with stories for my son's bedtime. My husband encouraged me to get my stories published, and so my journey began.

We are blessed with an extraordinary son, three dogs, and a fish. We have an amazing extended family who love and care for us dearly.

My hobbies include baking with my son, scrapbooking, reading, watching movies, and going on family walks.

God has given me so much, and I'm excited to see what other plans He has for me.

Copyright © 2024 by Brittany Gaddis Cummings

All rights reserved. No portion of this book may be copied or transmitted in any form, electronic or otherwise, without express written consent of the publisher or author.

Cover copyright © 2024 Seventh Star Press, LLC.

Illustrations: Designed by Freepik

Editor: Holly Phillippe

Published by Seventh StarChild

ISBN: 979-8-3305-5691-5

Seventh StarChild is an imprint of Seventh Star Press

www.seventhstarpress.com

info@seventhstarpress.com

Publisher's Note:

Learning About Loss is a work of fiction. All names, characters, and places are the product of the author's imagination, used in fictitious manner. Any resemblances to actual persons, places, locales, events, etc. are purely coincidental.

Printed in the United States of America

First Edition